Our Awesome GOD Made the World

LESLEY ROBBINS

Written and published by:
Lesley Robbins
E: lesrobbins57@gmail.com

Published March 2018 by Lesley Robbins

Page layout and publishing assistance:
Wild Side Publishing
wildsidepublishing.com
E: ray@thewildside.net

Proofread by Susi Hadassah

Cataloguing in Publication Data:
Title: Our Awesome God Made the World
ISBN: 978-0-473-43140-2 (pbk.)
ISBN: 978-0-473-43141-9 (ePub)
Subjects: Childrens, Christian Education, Bible stories

First printing 2018
International distribution Ingram Spark

Our Awesome
GOD
Made the World

Way back, before the very beginning, our awesome **God** was there. Then one day, before there was even a day, He spoke, *"Let there be light,"* and light appeared.
Then He spoke again, and the sky and the land appeared.
Next **God** spoke and the land was filled with trees and plants.

He spoke again and the sun, moon and stars came into being. Then He spoke and made fish to live in the water and animals to live on the land.

Lastly, **God** made man. He made man in His likeness. He made a man and a woman, so that they could get to know Him and keep Him company.

God looked at everything and saw how good it all was.

God had also created angels to serve Him, but one angel thought it was better than God and turned away and stopped serving Him.

One day the woman heard a voice that wasn't God's. The voice of the angel who had turned away from God, spoke through a crafty serpent.

He told the woman that she had misunderstood something that God had told her and the man. Because of what the serpent said, the woman made a mistake and did something that God told her not to do. The man also made the same mistake.

This damaged the wonderful relationship between **God** and the man and the woman. **God** had to do something, so He punished them.

The punishment was that they were sent out of the beautiful garden.

Things had become quite bad, because the man and woman's mistake had separated them, and everyone that came after them, from God.

However, God saw that a man named Noah had a good heart. He told Noah to build a boat. He was going to save Noah's family. God wanted two of every kind of animal to go into the boat with Noah, his wife, their three sons and their wives.

When Noah finished the boat, he took his family and the animals inside and shut the door. Then **God** sent rain. It rained so hard that the world was flooded and so the rain stopped.

When the flood waters finally dried up, Noah and his family went out to start the world again. The sin that entered the world, that very first time **God** was disobeyed, was still there.

But **God** didn't stop looking after people.

God had a plan that would take place many, many years in the future.

Many years after the flood, **God** saw another man that He knew would teach his family well. It was Abraham. There was only one problem. Abraham and his wife, Sarah didn't have any children.

Sarah thought she could fix this problem and Abraham had a son to one of her maids. But it wasn't what **God** wanted.

When **God** told Abraham that he would have a son, Sarah laughed. She did not think it was possible to have a baby now that she was very old. But Sarah discovered that nothing is impossible for **God!**

When Abraham and Sarah's baby was born, they called him Isaac. Through the story of Abraham and Isaac, God showed that one day, His Son would come into the world.

Many, many years later, God showed a man called Moses, ten things that were very important. The first thing was that people should love God first. He said He was the one and only true God.

They were not even to carve sticks or stones and think that they were anything like **God**. He said that people must never come before Him without seeing Him as **Holy**.

God said that there would be one special day each week, called the Sabbath. He wanted people to take a rest from their work, so that they could just love and be with Him.

God said that each person was to respect their own mother and father. No-one was to kill or commit adultery. No-one was to tell lies.

Lastly, God said that they were to be happy with the things that they had, instead of wanting what their neighbour had.

God wrote these ten things on stone and Moses carried them down the mountain to tell the people.

Through the years, **God** had people that listened to Him. Joshua, to whom he showed His power. David, who knew **God** and who slew Goliath.

Daniel, who He kept safe when he would not stop praying. There were many others who spoke and did things that **God** wanted them to say and do.

It was many years later that the time finally came for God to send His only Son into the world.

God saw a young woman named Mary, who lived in a small town called Nazareth, in Galilee. She was the one He chose to be the mother of His Son. God caused a baby to grow in her womb.

Mary, already engaged to Joseph, had to go to Bethlehem, because a census was being taken. When Mary and Joseph got to Bethlehem, the baby was born.

Jesus, **God's** son, was born in a stable, as there was no room at the inn. Shepherds out on the hillside, were given the good news by a host of angels.

Jesus grew up in Nazareth. When He was twelve years old, Mary and Joseph took Him to the temple in Jerusalem, for the Feast of Passover. But He didn't leave with the others, when it was time to return home.

His parents were worried, so they went back to look for Him. They found **Jesus** in the courts of the temple, talking with and listening to the men.

Jesus' words to them were,
"Didn't you think I would be about My Father's business?"

He went home with them and grew up well and strong.

When **Jesus** was 30 years old, He went to the river, Jordan.

His cousin, John the Baptist was baptising people in the river. John was telling everyone that there was One coming, who was from **God** and that His kingdom was drawing near.

Then suddenly, there He was. **Jesus** was at the river too.

John wanted to be baptised by Jesus. But, Jesus told John that He needed to be baptised by him. Then God's voice could be heard, as He said, *"This is my beloved Son, in whom I am well pleased."*

After He was baptised, Jesus went into the desert, where He was tempted by Satan. He overcame every temptation and then He went back to Nazareth. Everywhere Jesus went, He told everyone about God's kingdom. He healed people and performed miracles.

Jesus picked twelve men to be with Him. They watched Him as He taught and showed people everywhere, what **God's** kingdom is like.

Jesus forgave sins, healed the crippled and the blind, and raised the dead. He miraculously provided food more than once, and he also noticed that one day—when he healed ten people, only one came back to say thank you.

He saw deception, but He didn't come to judge. He came to help and He saw the hearts of those who were truly sorry for doing wrong.

Jesus helped people to understand, by telling parables. He showed them that, a simple act of kindness was better than a person thinking they were good. He said that, when one person was sorry for the things they had done and came back to **God**, the angels rejoiced.

And He told them not to waste the abilities **God** had given them.

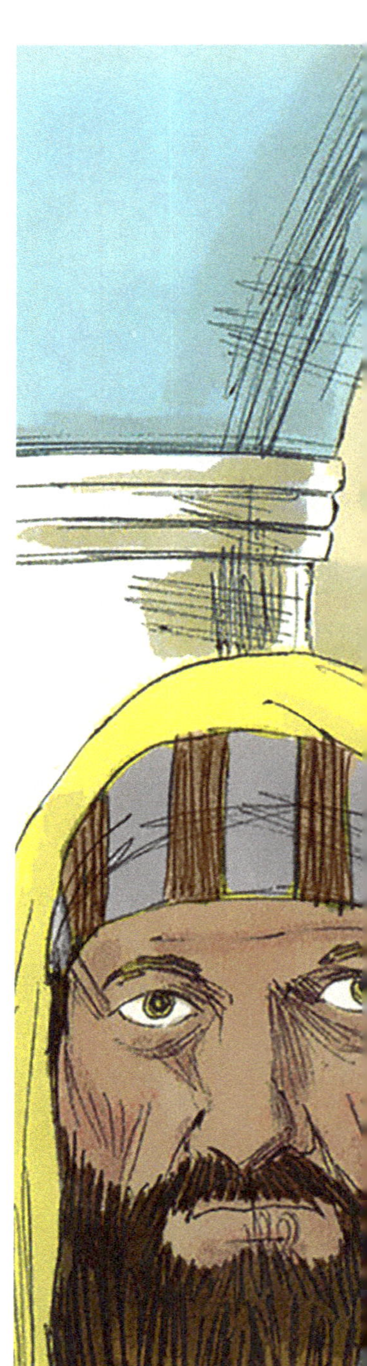

When **Jesus** had been with His disciples for three years, He knew His time had come. He was going to be betrayed. It was the time of the Passover Feast.

Jesus arranged to have a last supper with His disciples.

As they sat around the table, He took the bread that was a symbol of His body and broke it and shared it with them. Then He took the wine that stood for His blood and they all drank.

Jesus said that **God** was making a new promise.

Jesus' blood was about to be shed, so that everyone's sins could be forgiven.

Then **Jesus** went out into the garden. Soldiers came and arrested Him. He knew that **God**, His Father wanted Him to go with the soldiers. He was taken before a man called Pontius Pilate where they tried to find something to charge Him with.

When Pilate could find nothing wrong with Him, he asked the crowd that had gathered, to make a choice. It was his custom to allow one prisoner to go free.

So Pilate had Barabbas, a murderer, brought before them and asked them to choose between Barabbas and **Jesus**. The mob shouted *"Barabbas"*, so **Jesus** was sentenced to die.

As **Jesus** hung on the cross, darkness covered the land for three hours. When He died, the curtain in the temple ripped in half.

The way had been made, for mankind to come back to God. Three days after He died, Jesus came alive again. He had overcome death.

Before **Jesus** went back to Heaven, He appeared again to His disciples. He told them to wait until the **Holy Spirit** was sent from **God**.

They would then receive power to speak about **Jesus** in Jerusalem, Judea and to the ends of the earth. And that's what happened.

Today, why don't you ask **Jesus** to come into your heart and to take away your sins? Don't forget to say thank you, and tell **God** that you love Him.

He loves you!